Paws and Claws!

All about Foxes of the World
(Canids Family – Fox Edition)

Pet Books for Kids

Children's Biological Science of Dogs & Wolves Books

All Rights reserved. No part of this book may be reproduced or used in any way or form or by any means whether electronic or mechanical, this means that you cannot record or photocopy any material ideas or tips that are provided in this book.

Copyright 2016

Let's study about the elusive foxes. Why are they that mysterious?

They are all around us, but seem so distant from us.

Foxes are from the dog family. Wolves, grey foxes, raccoon dogs, and coyotes are their relatives.

It is believed that they originated in Europe, North Africa and Asia. In the mid-19th century, foxes were introduced to Australia.

Foxes usually live in a burrow underground. This is known as an 'earth'. But these creatures may also thrive in a cozy hollow above the ground, perhaps among the roots of a tree.

Foxes are highly adaptable animals. They can easily adjust to their surroundings.

They would most likely survive on any habitats available and sometimes very close to humans.

Although they are known as solitary animals, the males court and mate female foxes in winter.

The dog foxes, or male foxes, are like humans in supporting the vixen or female fox during the breeding season.

The males set out looking for food for the family. The family of a fox is called leash of foxes or skulk of foxes.

The vixen reproduces once a year with litters of one to 11 pups. The vixen faithfully protects and takes care of her pups. Foxes are indeed good parents.

The vixen or female fox is often assisted by a non-breeding sister in rearing her cub.

The non-breeding sister observes how the rearing is done and can apply her learned experiences when her time to breed comes.

About two weeks after being born, the cute cubs have their eyes and ears open. They venture out from the den when they are four weeksold.

They look like puppies with their short noses.

It is said that cubs die due to predators like badgers and dogs. But the motor vehicle is their worst known killer.

Hunger can also cause the death of these cubs. Foxes are quite amazing in their whiskers.

Yes, they have whiskers on their legs and around their faces.

It is believed that they use the whiskers as sensors to find their way when they're lost.

Foxes are great night hunters. They can see well at night like cats. They are active at night. Their eyes are adapted to night vision.

When light is shone into them at night, their eyes with vertical pupils glow green. They hunt their prey like cats. They do it by stalking and pouncing.

How do they eat their food? Do they chew their food like us?

Foxes use their shearing teeth or carnassials to cut the meat into chunks and then swallow the chunks down. They do not chew their food.

Foxes really have a lot in common with cats. They have spines on their tongue. They walk with elegance in a cat-like tread.

Moreover, like cats, foxes can climb trees with their retractable claws. They also settle and sleep on low branches like cats. Foxes are hunted for their fur.

Their tails are cutoff and serve as trophies for hunters. The fox tail is called a brush. The most common among the foxes is the red fox.

Red fox are adaptive in many environments due to their flexible diet, and they have the widest geographical range. Foxes, just like birds and turtles, use the earth's magnetic field to hunt food.

Kids, foxes are highly sociable. Foxes are known to be playful, fun and curious. They play among themselves and with other animals like cats and dogs.

Have you imagined yourself playing with a fox?

That could be a nice experience.

Made in the USA
Middletown, DE
26 November 2017